MUSINGS OF A BODACIOUS BARD

THE SPARK THAT IGNITES, LIVES WITHIN YOU

ANSHUMAN SHARMA

Made with ♥ on the Notion Press Platform
www.notionpress.com

To my grandfather,

For imbibing in me a love for literature and classical novels at a very early age and teaching me never to stop dreaming. This endeavor would be impossible without your love and guidance.

Contents

Contents

Contents

Contents

Foreword

It is my honor and privilege to introduce you to the poetry of Anshuman Sharma, a dear friend and a truly gifted poet. When Anshuman writes, his words take on a life of their own, weaving together in ways that are both powerful and mesmerizing.

As you read through the pages of this collection, you will discover the depth and range of Anshuman's poetic voice. From romantic to mysterious, from motivational to serene, his poems capture a wide range of emotions and experiences. Through his vivid imagery and evocative language, Anshuman invites us to see the world in a new way and to explore the beauty and wonder that surround us.

What strikes me most about Anshuman's poetry is his ability to connect with his readers on a personal level. His words speak directly to the heart, tapping into our deepest hopes, fears, and desires. Whether he is exploring the beauty of nature or the complexities of the human spirit, Anshuman's poetry has the power to move and inspire us.

I hope that you will take the time to savor each poem in this collection, to let Anshuman's words wash over you and transport you to a world of imagination and wonder. I am confident that you will come out of this experience with a deeper appreciation for the art of poetry and a newfound admiration for the talent of Anshuman Sharma.

Khushi Katyal

Preface

Poetry has always been a way to express myself and connect with the world around me. Over the years, I have filled countless notebooks with my thoughts, observations, and musings, each reflecting my journey as a writer and a person.

The poems encapsulated in this collection are a culmination of that journey, spanning many years and experiences. Some are deeply personal, drawn from my own life and emotions. Others are inspired by the people and places I have encountered on my travels. And some are simply exercises in language and form, experiments in the art of poetry itself.

What ties these poems together is a common thread of wonder and curiosity, a desire to explore the mysteries of life and the world we live in. I hope readers will find something of themselves in these pages, whether it is in the joy of a new discovery, the ache of a lost love, or the wonder of a starry night sky.

Writing poetry is a solitary pursuit, but it is also a way of connecting with others. I am grateful for the many friends, family members, and fellow poets who have supported me and the readers who will now take these words into their hearts and minds.

Thank you for joining me on this journey.

Anshuman Sharma

Acknowledgements

Writing poetry can be a lonely and challenging pursuit, but it is also deeply rewarding. I am grateful for the many people who have supported me along the way, offering encouragement, feedback, and inspiration when I needed it most.

First and foremost, I want to thank my family for their unwavering support and love. Without their encouragement, I would never have pursued my passion for writing, and this book would not exist.

I extend my gratitude to my girlfriend, who urged me to nurture my literary acumen and weave magic through my words. My mentor, who I am really grateful towards, saw this spark of words in me and pushed me to write consistently. I also want to thank my new friends who have listened to my poems and provided valuable feedback and support. Your kindness and encouragement have meant the world to me.

To my fellow poets and writers, thank you for inspiring me with your work and offering me the guidance and advice that have helped me improve my writing.

Finally, I want to thank the readers who will take these poems into their lives and hearts. It is an honor to share my words with you, and I hope they will bring you joy, comfort, and inspiration.

Anshuman Sharma

Prologue

Poetry is a way of seeing the world, capturing the beauty and complexity of life in a single line or stanza. It is a way of distilling the essence of our experiences into something that can be shared and connect us with others and with ourselves.

In this collection of poems, I have tried to capture some of the moments, emotions, and thoughts that have moved me over the years. Some of these poems are personal, drawn from my life and experiences. Others are more ubiquitous, exploring themes that we all grapple with at one time or another.

But they all will connect with you in some way or the other. Whether you are a lover of poetry or a newcomer to the art form, my goal is to create a space for reflection, introspection, and joy. I want these poems to compel you to take a breath to savor the beauty of language and the power of human expression.

Of course, poetry is also a deeply personal art form, and what resonates with one person may not resonate with another. That is okay. I hope you find something in these pages that speaks to you, moves you, and makes you see the world in a new light.

So, welcome to my world of poetry. Let us explore it together, one word at a time.

Anshuman Sharma

1. O Come All, Ye Faithful

O come all, ye faithful,
In glee, you bow to whom?
A fellow begs for shelter –
For whom you spare no room,
Funny, you know not this fellow –
Could he be who grants all boon?
In this bliss of ignorance –
You sail shallow waters,
"Faith is enough," you lie to self –
And do so to thy sons and daughters,
An exalted faith when nurtured wrong –
Has time and again showered slaughters.
I believe in thee, yet, and so I say –
O come all, ye faithful,
In glee, I shall bow with you,
Bow and pledge to be grateful,
We have tons, yet generosity is rare,
Bow and pledge to be fairly gainful,
For the one who sees and knows all –
Of bad faith is surely hateful.

2. The Unheeded

Day in and day out,
This wallflower goes unheeded.
While the world around him went arrogantly about,
A "Hey, how's it going?" was all he needed.
To his teacher's pet moment, they would pout at him,
But at least, in their way, they now greeted him.
The youngest in the family, highly protected,
Never putting his foot down was what he regretted.
(Un)Intentionally tackled in the hallway,
Not even a "sorry," would they say.
But the fire in his soul kept him going,
Through the sea of hideous brats, rowing and rowing.
Always picked last by either of the team,
To which the other team would celebrate their "obvious" win.
They all failed to see in him his gleam,
Oh, they are going to regret their sin.

3. One Last Gift

She found it in the corner of her basement,
A beautiful thing covered in webs and dust.
Lying amongst the musty artifacts and peeled-off cement,
Like a woman married without consent, unable to adjust.
This beautiful thing was finally discovered,
For it seemed to have waited too long.
If only things could talk, we'd know how it suffered,
Perhaps the same way its painter did, who was now long gone.
With her shivering hands and soul-shivering self, she wiped off the dirt,
For she sensed a familiarity with the painter at first.
It was her mother, a ridiculous painter,
But to her, it did not matter.
She loved those colorful moments together,
That was all that would matter.
A pack a day was casually burnt,
The addiction her mother could never resist.
Long after burying her, now she learned,
This painting she left behind was the one last gift.

4. The Barren Bricks Speak

I have seen them tear each other apart,
For reasons ridiculously unreasonable.
The fate of this land was sealed from the start,
"War Zone" is the label stuck with me.
I was a place breeding life, food, and air,
For the good, generous, and grateful enough.
Look at me now in gloom and despair,
The once softest flowers lay here crippled and rough.
The fallen braves on the dents of this earth,
Was it worth the nameless precious lives?
Unlikely it is here now for anything to take birth,
Could reparations ever be made for those martyrs' wives?
I stand here unaware of the sin I committed,
For I was the chosen one to witness this omen.
Those alive in bits and pieces lay admitted,
Thinking about their fellow fallen men.
Now the sun scarcely shines,
Life is petrified to find a way.
Amongst the lifeless barks and vines,
The only color I see now is grey.

5. Blue Beads

Reminisces, over time, –
We bind by the piece,
Each bead bound, bears –
With it some memories,
The thread that holds –
Could break with ease.
This necklace you keep safe,
Hidden from all, even you,
A spark in the present ignites –
And brews a nostalgic view,
And so, scatters all beads,
Some, you realize, are blue.
Numbly, at first, you gaze,
Heart briskly beats at the bead,
It unfolds itself to whisk you –
To what you vowed to pay no heed,
"What differently could I have done?"
This quandary makes your heart bleed.
The rain stops, alas –
And its bow you now see,
Peace with them you have made,
You smile at the beads' debris,
Wear, in pride, this necklace now,
Without the blue, one is not esprit.

6. Wuthering Junctures

Idle, cozy, in your zone,
Blood numbs on your bones,
Wearing on you a torpid cologne,
Lollygags you blindly condone,
If wish not to be a workaday clone —
One step today would aid you to atone,
Wuthering junctures you shall face,
But against them, you are a cyclone.
The air alters not,
But somehow feels thin,
Status shifts time and again,
Like a snake sheds its skin,
Congruous steps every day,
In due time your world shall spin,
Wuthering junctures come forth,
Some you lose, some you win,
For through these qualms —
One nurtures a strong chin.

7. Buried Boulevard

Artifacts, pricey, presented –
On these streets, so vibrant,
Centuries before, perhaps, stood –
Here the home of a migrant,
Eons before even that, perhaps –
This housed a fearsome tyrant.
Wonder once, as you wander –
The streets for a desire stirred,
What must it have been like,
The bygone buried boulevard?
A grandson sees a see-saw –
As a nostalgic tear touches the ground,
A family once here rejoiced,
A well, so fine, majestically crowned.
One may or may not heed,
To do so, there is no need,
But for the buried boulevards –
There may be some who'd gladly bleed.

8. The Sixth Shot

With a pride like none –
I entered the field,
In my mind –
My victory was sealed,
The first ball, so harsh,
The truth it revealed.
Taken aback,
But still in pride,
A second strike,
I failed, but tried.
The third one launched,
The fear in me swelled,
My wits and fists I gripped –
As in my hands my bat I held,
Once again, I faced a strike,
I stand here, perplexed and spelled.
The hope in me dilutes,
The light within descends to dark,
As came the fourth one,
Into an abyss, I disembarked.
I cursed and loathed myself,
A humble wave shattered the glass,
The glass of pride, indeed, is thin,
'Twas this pride that I ought to surpass.

The fifth one I missed again,
I took this fall in a better way,
A learning curve; this time, I saw,
In the dark abyss, I saw a new day.
The one in front tried again –
To kick me down once again,
My calm self I did maintain,
In haste, nothing you obtain,
A last chance, toward me, gained,
The shot I took was not in vain,
The five I missed I thought were bane,
But a mind so sane it helped me attain.

9. Let Go

A time comes often –
When you need to let go,
Let go of the shackles –
On you that grow and grow.
Holding you back –
From all you could be,
Clumsy and reckless,
But to learn, be free.
Beneath these shackles –
Rests your wings,
The branch you're stuck on,
Fear is what it will bring,
The weight of the shackles –
Sting and Sting,
Break them and trust your wings,
The fall is pretty while you swing,
A time will surely come –
When atop heavens, you'd be aswing.

10. For a Paradise, Unprepared

Catapulted to the sky,
A trip to heaven, perhaps,
Knew not how badly –
Into an abyss, I'd collapse,
A paradoxical tinge I did feel –
For a paradise so bliss could have many traps,
But, nonetheless, for a wee moment –
I let go of all my straps,
'Twas my biggest mistake,
I lost my home's maps,
A smooth launch, oh so bliss,
On my way took many naps,
I touched the moon at last,
And so began to cruelly relapse,
"Who was I even kidding?"
This thing, now, constantly slaps,
To even walk now, I feel scared,
I lost so many of my flaps,
To give up or not on another venture –
This conundrum constantly taps,
Perhaps there shall come one day –
When all these taps turn into claps,

The moon I touched, but unprepared,
But it would be great to enjoy the Alps.

11. I May Not See Tomorrow

Scathed so long –
With a lost touch,
Being abandoned –
Is a pain too much,
What began as a marathon –
Is now limping with a crutch.
Licking your wounds –
Day in and day out,
Wondering and wandering –
Feeding your self-doubt,
If one fine day –
Would rain bless your drought?
A few kicks it takes –
To revive an enveloped bike,
A walk a day it may take –
To carry on your heroic hike.
So, today's walk to myself I owe,
For I may end up not seeing a tomorrow.

12. A Ride off the Cliff

Blocked breaths, vision blurred,

Atop a peak, nary a voice heard,

"Commitment" is the paramount word —

No matter how badly you're injured,

Seeing you thrive, they'll call you absurd,

But among penguins, you'll be a real bird.

Atop the peak, you stand proud, in glee,

Enjoy the view that only you can see,

Gazing as far as the eye can see,

Do peer back to a prodigious journey.

Although you may once fall,

One never sees the devil's squall,

Its sadism hopes you rue and recall —

Your hellish hike and its copious brawls,

But, rather enjoy this beautiful fall,

Laugh at the face of this inept squall,

It's only a fall if you let it enthrall,

Release your wings and fly atop tall.

13. Twenty-Fifty

Welcome to the twenty-fifty,
Look around yourself.
The price the past has paid is hefty,
But a room can broom itself.
Cars can take you anywhere,
Who needs a driver now?
Plants of plastic here and there,
Don't need a farmer to plough.
Welcome to the twenty-fifty,
Try not to be scared.
Accountants who were then so shifty,
Are now "obsolete" declared.
They pay for and raise metals,
Kids and pets are less and less.
It knows all from ketchup to kettles,
Can do all from cook to press.
Welcome to the twenty-fifty,
I know it's hard to process.
You were an employee pretty and nifty,
But this thing can do it in less.
Delivery persons, millions such,
That humane touch you miss?
This thing, for that, gives heed not much,
But it's unlikely for it to be amiss.

Welcome to the twenty-fifty,
How creative can you be?
It's the age of the swift and flinty,
Your creativity can take a knee.
The sun barely shines or sets,
For the gods are now dubious.
The heavens often play their bets,
To know the date of "The End,"
They are all so curious!

14. Better Luck Next Time

Do you feel the floor shaking?
Is the air around getting thinner?
Do you see the windows breaking?
Is everyone around now a sinner?
Are the oceans hugging the lands?
Are the mountains breathing fire?
Do the cracks on earth continue to expand?
Or did your catastrophically beautiful mind,
Once again, a rotten taste it went to acquire?
Look at me and everything around,
What it was yesterday is now not the same.
One thing lost, but a million found,
Good riddance! For the lost was lame.
Chaos Theory is your motto,
Experimentation is your foe.
Preaching from your grotto,
How do you expect me to grow?
You "believe in me", but conditionally,
The comfortably cocooning conditions.
I rather seek to unleash unconventionally,
To boldly board on minacious missions.
The spikes of uncertainty no more hurt,
They're wielded rather as a weapon now.
Let your guards down and your hands in the dirt,

For the armors of the past are of no use now.
Though you're not to blame,
But your visions are finite.
Within me is this raging flame,
Which'll light what's beyond infinite.
Your fearful refusal, my stubborn zeal,
Between us, these sands of time.
Haters lean forth to my fall, but I heal,
To them, I say, "Better luck next time."

15. A Stranger in the Mirror

As I gaze into the mirror –
A stranger is all I see,
The man meant to be himself –
Is now a pile of dispiriting debris.
Boulders of hopes and expectations –
From everyone but him, he carries,
Letting go of them and being his own –
To him is an endeavor so scary.
A pity pat of validation –
Is enough for his worth,
But to please a hollow world –
Is not why he took birth.
Day in and day out –
I gaze at the mirror in hope,
In hope of recognizing the man in it,
For I believe, in him, there is scope,
Scope to abscond the societal tags –
And with his true self, he shall elope.

16. Ghosts of the Past

Why thee haunt me —
Again and again,
My endeavors to push you —
Are rendered moot, in vain,
Rearing, often, your ugly heads,
Nary a reason, what do you gain?
Purely evil and sadistic —
You feed off my misery and pain.
You do not belong here,
You are a thing of the past,
A part of me I wish not to face,
For you are a thing aghast.
But pushing you does no good,
You simply strike back harder,
Perhaps I ought to hear you out —
And thaw your foulness with ardor.
Think me not an enemy, oh ghosts of the past,
Confide in me, and in peace we shall last.

17. One Who Loves Your Flaws

A crooked nose –
Or even without one,
Dumb, deaf, or blind,
Never will she ever shun,
Such is the love of a mother –
That would live until lives the sun.
It matters not how bright you shine,
Your worth, your wealth does not define,
And even at times when she was low –
She would tend to your every whim and whine.
Pity to those who undervalue –
The one who loves your every flaw,
This world makes you freeze in cold,
It is her love that can make it thaw.

18. Sweet Home Indeed

The first morsel early morning,
I had forgotten its sweet taste,
Rushing for something or the other,
To eat thrice, I'd ignore in haste.
To worry not of my health,
Here my mother does it best,
Carefree, in my home –
I unapologetically roam and rest.
I need never a shield,
I fence with danger with ease,
But my father behind my back –
Each day I fearlessly cease.
'Tis only when I left for more –
I understood what I left behind,
Now I am here, for a little while –
I wish somehow, I could be confined.

19. A Dip Amidst the Greatness

A height once reached,
On a path to something great,
A liability comes along —
That can make or break your fate.
A fate that you don't know,
But you work for it anyway,
'Tis a thing of greatness,
Trust with patience is the only way.
Hanging on to that rope,
It's not a task so easy,
'Tis on you to break through the storm —
Or whisk back to a life, lame and breezy.

20. Ode to the Old

Take me home,
Oh, rough road,
The old awaits –
'Tis indeed gold,
I've seen so much so soon,
Classic warmth I am owed.
Amidst the cold –
That I myself chose,
Leaving behind my armor –
For the real me to expose,
The excitedly bold –
Now can't feel his toes.
Amidst this wilderness –
A new me I have found,
What once went unheard,
Many a people I now astound,
Despite me loving this new –
I wish for the old to surround.
'Tis perhaps a dip,
That every larva feels –
Before it unleashes –
And its blazing beauty it reveals.
Day in and day out –
I'm getting closer to me,

I'm enjoying the growth –
That comes with being free,
But amidst the conquered clouds
I miss my mother's serene glee.
Take me home –
Oh, rough road,
The proud me –
Wishes to unload,
For a wee moment –
I wish to hold –
Onto those stories –
As a child I was told.

21. A Heal Deserved

This child you rear has no flesh –
But, could at times get hurt,
At times it stumbles –
And falls into the dirt.
This child is naive,
It knows nary a pit,
Annoying it is, often,
But on this child, don't quit,
For the day you put a ring on your mate -
You both swore to do your bit.
The bond born that day -
Is precious and pure,
Life's precarious ailments -
Its divine nature can cure.
To live, you need not rear this,
But colorless is life without this child,
Tiny endless efforts from both ends -
Can make your time on earth beguiled.

22. Name to Fame

One is born with it,

Who gives birth, gives this too,

The name they call you with –

Make people know, more than a few.

One is born with a choice,

A choice to make or not,

A choice to purvey their name,

Or until death let it clot.

How one is born matters not,

How one lives decides their fate,

From name to fame is tedious,

Many, however, can not relate.

To break the walls that restrict,

'Tis a task needing a strong will,

Start one day and resume till the end,

'Tis not a one-day kill,

But this journey is one truly great,

Open to all who aim for that thrill.

23. A Beautiful Bonus

'Tis not something you need,
You, yourself, are adequate,
But a partner for life, to be with,
'Tis what makes your life ornate.
Bestowing burdens of our needs —
On one who truly loves us,
If they succeed, we love them back,
Or else we resent or cuss,
Another being deserves not this,
For in our lives, they're just a plus.
A stipend or a salary,
'Tis a thing that stays same,
We work harder for a bonus —
To live not a life lame.
Appreciate and care for this,
But we ought not to lean on it,
This beautiful bonus is a delicate thing,
Maintain it, and your life it shall never quit.

24. Alone Amidst All

Soaked all night, now dry,
I open to the piercing rays,
Such a cunning rippling start,
It has been more than a few days.
'Tis not a thing to dwell on,
But I feel more than some,
I have seen myself ripped apart –
And lay torn, terrified, and numb.
I had heard of others like me,
Those who met the same fate,
On their body, thousands had fought,
War, bred by lust and hate.
Barren lands like myself –
Lay alone amidst all,
Parts of us are still red –
Where green trees once stood tall,
Uprooted to make space for the dead,
Lifeless friends I now enthrall.

25. Will, the Wishing Well

Standing on the edge –
Of a generous wishing well,
Innocently, I put my hope,
And then wait and dwell.
I wait for my wish to come true,
I see so many do the same,
Throw a Hail Mary –
For all the wealth and fame.
'Tis a generous well,
But 'tis not one that you can see,
I'm standing next to an empty well –
Which would listen not to any plea.
"The well you desire is within you,"
Said the wisest of the wise,
Through thy will, you reach the goal,
'Tis the only way to rise.

26. Light and Dark

The absence of light –
To appreciate the dark,
A melodious chime –
After a vicious bark.
A Tale of Woe –
Of two lost lives,
But they meet at last –
In the heaven's hive.
To recognize the sweet –
One ought to know the sour,
The beaten down knows what's weak –
So, they value what is true power.
Nature bestows both,
Beyond the dark, there is light,
They both are needed, for –
The dawn is empty without the night.

27. Diminished

Into my chest, he plunged –
His hands, to rip my heart,
For a while, it kept searching,
Nary a flinch nor a blart.
The demon of hell, perplexed –
When his hand came out empty,
The heart's chamber was a void,
Subjugation, it had gone through plenty.
'Tis a thing that shrinks the heart,
It pumps less, as it's curbed more,
So harshly it had been curbed, and –
Detached from all the good and pure,
Such that the demon would cry,
For it saw a man worse than impure.

28. In the Dark

Amidst the darkness –
He ignited a bright light,
Nary a one could see –
Within him, a ferocious fight,
When the whole world slept –
He made minacious moves in the night.
They wish not to see him work,
They are in awe when he buds out,
For all his dreams and their blows –
He worked like a true devout.
For all that he began,
For all that he was let down,
Breaking all the odds –
He walks now with a graceful crown.
Through the alley, so dark,
Within him, a blustery spark,
On the hook of consistency –
On this earth, he made his mark.

29. Incomplete

Empty still, I would feel —
Times when I'd see me,
Seeking myself out in others,
Like a fruitless petite tree.
Like a pup wiggles its tail —
To its master's gentle pat,
A simple validating praise,
Jovially, I would go flat.
I'd go to great lengths —
For meaningless applauds —
From the ones I know barely,
'Tis a gamble against the odds,
For the world is filled with those —
Who'd call those like me clods.
Incomplete, all the way,
For I easily would sway,
When the lotus cares not of the swamp —
Hope shall shine on it that day.

30. Passionately Needed

Passionately, I needed this,
A day to rejuvenate,
To make choices, perhaps bad,
But the tensity within would extirpate.
Nary a heed to the musts,
What's necessary shall be done,
With time the musts settle –
And in the end, it matters none.
During the second to last breath –
The only thing we'd wonder –
A dull life, and now death,
Could've done some beautiful blunders.
A break, rest, or a needed pause,
I chose to listen to my heart,
A much-needed choice it was,
Next morning would be a strong restart.

31. Sail Somehow

Broken legs? Crawl,
Limbs give up but stand tall,
This fight is yours, you fighter,
Back down not from a brawl.
The sail ahead is rough,
But it knows not you're tough,
There comes a time —
When enough is enough.
That time is now,
How many times will you bow?
The world spits on the weak,
To the weak turned around, at last, they bow.
A path to your flame, you allow,
With will and zeal, yourself endow,
Together with some or even alone —
The rough sail, sail somehow.

32. My Own Space

Amidst the crowd,
Their sound so loud,
Within my space, I stay —
And work for what I vowed.
To the rest, it matters not,
But my work shall not rot,
Many would resist and curse —
And try to loosen your knot.
This thing gives an impetus —
To go about this world of cuss,
With a smile on your face —
And in thy soul a grace.
My own space I would not trade,
With tears and sweat, this, I made,
In a world so fast and hassled —
A while with my space, my soul would aid.

33. For Eons to Come

The sun shall shine as it does,
Same old conundrum and fuss,
For aeons to come, of our love –
The one who cared would surely buzz.
'Tis not one to come often,
What we share can't be forgotten,
A bond so strong that minstrels pledge,
So pure that the devil would soften.
Many a hater we have seen,
To break us apart, many are keen,
But so far, we have sailed smoothly –
For on each other, we confide and lean.
Like a warm hug amidst the snow,
You hold me tight so I don't flow,
I held your hand, never to let go,
'Tis a promise, I want you to know,
Together strong we shall grow,
Through the storm, we'll gallantly row.

34. The Fall

The fall, so beautiful,
Limbs lost in the air,
A feeling of being free –
Of which you dearly care.
In that moment –
When your resistance wins –
And further fuels it,
You excuse all your sins.
A thing you began with zeal,
A zeal and will to not let go,
To care for that thing every day –
Whether you're jovial or low.
The fall so blissfully beautiful,
'Tis the landing that hurts,
But to get back up and resume,
The thing you care for, it reasserts.

35. Cold Numbing Aid

Not a single flinch,
The soul so serenely surreal,
Beyond a time, it matters not —
What is fake and what is real.
A rug so warm —
Amidst all the qualms,
I've brushed under it —
Many a mental storm.
With a head held high —
I face the world, sane,
With a smile on my face —
I show not an ounce of pain.
The pain subsides over time —
With this cold numbing aid,
But feeling all that is good —
Is the price that I paid.

36. A Toxic Feed

A cry for help –
That goes unheard,
Open palms surfacing the lake,
From those watching, not a single word.
None to blame,
Yet all to blame,
For a dew of hope –
Could put out the flame.
Futile move 'tis at times –
To expect someone to show up,
Knocked down by the hollow apologies,
You yourself would be fed up.
"Helpless and hopeless",
Never must you dwell.
Brace up to this woeful world,
Stop feeding an empty well,
'Tis you alone and your guts –
Who can whisk you out from any hell.

37. Uncocooned

'Tis what can't be tamed,
A change is inevitable,
All his life a horse —
Can not rust in its stable.
For better or for worse,
It matters not which way —
Goes the needle of change,
What awaits, only time can say.
But one can turn the wheels of time,
Resisting the resistance itself,
To do what indeed scares them —
And break out of their safe shell.
A snake sheds its skin to grow,
Upon you, let life bestow —
For all your bends and cracks —
An unmatched unique glow.

38. What Does it Take

The cringing of the soul –
To its cunning sudden slap,
A slap followed by the wave –
Of memory, in which we woefully wrap.
What does it take to get it out?
What does it take to move on?
Move on from those memories –
That make it tough to face the dawn.
Time slows down,
Taking its own time –
To mock our every effort,
The hill in front is tough to climb.
'Tis a funny thing,
'Tis only time that tells –
The day you shall move on,
Move on from this heinous hell.

39. Assisting Thy Will

'Tis beyond difficult –
To extirpate a leech –
Latched on to you by you,
To get it off, daily you preach.
You preach and plead, but –
Succumb back to it,
One after another –
Those fags keep getting lit,
And upon closing your eyes –
On sand you write "I'll quit".
Your will is strong,
It knows what's wrong,
Its efforts to whisk you out –
Deserves not to prolong.
Assist your will,
It keeps you from the leech's kill,
Burning a fag to burn yourself –
It truly is an abhorrent thrill.

40. A Land in Despair

I walked past the land –
Who cried a heinous havoc,
A havoc ignited by greed,
Receiving less, some don't stomach.
This land saw slaughters,
Men slicing those unknown,
Nary a bounty would they taste,
These men, the aristocrats owned.
Why and how it sparked?
Perhaps it could have calmed,
Less than greed if they'd accept –
Countless lives could've been unharmed.
I walked past the land in despair,
Vultures feeding upon the precious,
These lives laid down, 'twas not worth,
If only the powerful were more gracious.

41. Wise Learnings

Wrongs were done,
Not every old is gold,
We realise the unfair,
The past, when we radically unfold.
The wise were so,
We blindly follow,
To those who are "wise" –
Questions are tough to swallow.
Follow not blindly,
You have the right to ask,
The inquisitiveness within –
Never let it mask.
The ones born before –
Have certainly seen more,
Receive their wise learnings,
But have a mind of your own.

42. Lovely Loneliness

It bothers not,
The damning silence,
For there's peace —
In its eerie essence.
Alone all around,
This surreal place,
In its cold warmth —
I find a serene solace.
At times such —
I feel alien,
But I forget not —
I'm a lonely lion.
An assurance it gives me,
With myself, I can be,
Nary a one do I need,
In solitude, I can be free.

43. Empty Calls

How elated she'd feel –
When her phone would ring,
My name displayed,
So merrily she'd sing.
With time we grow,
With life's to-and-fro,
Losing touch with a loved one –
Along with life's unfair flow.
A mother's love, incomparable,
On her phone, I cannot ring,
My ring would not be received,
Among the angels, she now sings.

44. Worth

On the days you wonder –
If 'tis even worth,
The thing you work for every day,
The thing to which you gave birth.
Not every day does it pay,
Not every day you would care,
But even on such days –
To pay no heed is not fair.
On such days, when you feel low,
On such days, when the day is slow,
It takes a mighty soul –
To keep up the precious flow.
It is you who chose –
To commence a challenging venture,
Along with the bounties –
You receive hurdles on any adventure.

45. Serene Solitude

Carry me, o wind,
To a place unknown,
Unknown to the mass –
So, I'm blissfully alone.
A place that's all pure,
Most ill that shall cure,
Away from all the impure –
I'd love to live, for sure.
Take me, o wind,
You're the one I lean on,
For here amongst all –
I feel like a surreal swan.
To be a part and belong,
'Tis for which we all long,
In a serene solitude, however,
Lies my melancholically merry song.

46. Unwell in a Well

I stand on the edge –
Of a well, so bewitching,
Why would one want out?
Leaving behind the snug and cozy,
Reach great height, but twitching.
The ones within this well,
A life so warm they live,
Of the world beyond these walls –
Nary a heed they give.
Marinating in their shell,
Within a limit, do they jell,
Only when it is too late –
On their warmth do they dwell.
I gaze down this well –
Pitying the ones who smile,
A view of the world I have seen –
When I boarded a minacious mile.

47. Lived on Forever

They dug for a while,
On a soil, abandoned,
Abandoned like those two, who –
The haters of love shunned.
How far does one go –
For what they wish to live?
Love, the strongest of them all,
Their soul people jovially give.
It matters hardly,
Shunned or not,
True love thrives –
While their haters rot.
They dug deep into the soil,
They knew not what they'd find,
Years later, on a soil abandoned –
Was found an epitome, entwined,
Entwined were the bones of the two,
Even in death, their bond is enshrined.

48. A Taste Much Needed

I miss all that I knew –
On this land so new,
Alone here, on my wits,
For this life, I was due.
A taste of this freedom,
Like a hot stick on something numb,
A cocooned curious child,
Now building his own kingdom.
I left the soft and warm,
Now among a surreal swarm,
But an exceptional eruption –
Needs something to deform.
Few are such who receive –
An opportunity to achieve,
Achieve what's always hidden within,
And so in their excellence, they'd believe.

49. It Happens for Sure

Your blood and sweat –
Shed for your desires,
The conquered chasms,
The whole world it inspires.
You work and pray –
Day and night,
The universe delivers –
What is your right.
With a gallant heart –
You make your moves,
The honest efforts –
Your outcome proves.
The soul-shattering brawls,
The blocks you endure,
A sweet fruit you'll reap,
It happens for sure.

50. It's Okay to Live

It hurts less and less,
The wounds given to myself,
Each passing day, it stings,
For my soul is in a shelf.
I curb the waves within –
With a dam built over time,
At times they screech and crawl,
Over this dam, they wish to climb.
A havoc they would wreak –
If the dam turns weak,
To save all that is precious –
Of this silence, I continue the streak.
But these wounds hurt less,
A relief to myself, I do not give,
Under these hills of subjugation –
I forgot it's okay to live.

51. Along With You

In your arms, all along,
No where else do I belong,
To a place so serene and warm —
Let's head and sing our merry song.
None shall hound,
Free from all bounds,
Just you and me,
Safe and sound.
I care not for the grand,
With your hand in my hand —
I tour all of heaven —
Which otherwise is a barren land.
Precious moments with you,
Our love for us so true,
Tasteless terrible morsels —
Taste sweet along with you.

52. Meet you There

Shed no tear on my grave,
Those moments we spent, save,
I know not where I'm headed –
But of this world, I'm no more a slave.
Glad to have spent such time,
Times, some tough, some sublime,
Lots of moments fulfilled,
Some still in grime.
It matters no more,
I have already left the shore,
Regrets, I have none, but –
Leaving you behind a hole it would bore.
All your love and care,
Affection that is so rare,
Nary a thing can I do, but –
Where I am headed, I shall meet you there.

53. Bow Not

The stream against you —
With all its might and rage,
A chapter so brutal, But —
You shall soon turn the page,
Until such time comes —
One ought to boldly engage,
For the stream against you —
Stops not until one's back in a cage.
The cage that one finally broke,
That's step one to stepping off your cloak,
The cloak which kept one safe and sound —
But the world thought of them as a joke.
Mighty respect to one —
Who cuts off this knot,
The stream shall strangle you,
But whatever it takes, bow not,
For those who cross this stream —
On the hall of fame, there's their spot.

54. A Man Child's Day Out

I recall the shelves being full,
I recall all things being there,
A brat, not spoilt but fresh,
Always under his parent's care.
Of the hustle behind every morsel —
I knew nary a thing,
I traipsed through the store's stalls,
How to my mother I wished to cling.
But a voice within so proud,
Proud of me for faring through —
Like an adult, which I am,
Of this life, I was due.
A man-child's day out,
I believe in myself now —
More than I ever did before,
I know more of the what and how.

55. Dull Dry Day

Times such often come –
When you'd simply gaze –
At a noxious nothingness,
For the soul seems stuck in a haze.
A haze of perplexed,
Life, dull as the grey sky,
Takes tons of might to get up –
And get through this day so dry.
To curl up in a shell –
Is a way out, easy,
But come what hell –
One should be not sleazy.
This day is perhaps a test,
This dreary, dull, dry day,
Hold on tight and survive –
And so receive, for what you pray.

56. Kept On

I stopped for none,
I greeted back none,
I kept on walking –
A monotonous marathon.
A life of regrets,
On a single path, I was set,
Went above and beyond –
To repay all my debts.
Of family, friends, or even foe –
Less than acquaintance I know,
On this path, I paid heed to none,
Went along the stream's flow.
In search of my fate,
Fearing I would be late,
Moments, precious, I lost,
I stand now at heaven's gate.

57. The Tune

A tune hummed, familiar,
It took me to where I belonged,
A place so close and known,
For its taste I deeply longed.
This tune, so cunningly calm,
I was vastly aware of the new,
The new where I ought to belong,
But I crave the place where I grew.
A sudden hit of reality,
A sudden hit of apprehension,
I had not absorbed the new,
A feeling of being shunned.
This mesmerizingly melancholic tune,
I knew not what to think,
Stood still, I gazed into nothingness –
Until my teary eyes blinked.

58. A Descent from Heaven

The roars died down,
They dropped their arms,
The bloodshed paused –
To her mysterious charms.
With an aura of one –
Descended from heaven,
In the darkness, a beautiful sun,
Such was she, among these men.
These men who care for none –
Until they realize that they care,
Through her, they saw their humanity,
For in her, they saw someone they care,
A mother, a wife, a daughter, or a sister –
Each got to see their respective share.
And so, the war concluded,
Loved ones are weeping at home –
A descent from the heaven showed,
The ground was cleared by gloam.

59. A Friend with Fins

I saw a smiling fish,
A tiny crescent on its face,
Among the others, in a tank,
Like angels floating in space.
I saw it involved in itself,
Nary a world's worry,
No predator to abscond from –
Or run for its life in a scurry.
How beautiful a piece of being,
How delicately precious it is,
On this land, so new to me –
Its serene smile sucked me from abyss.
An abyss of reminiscence,
The wheels of nostalgia and time,
A new place, however great –
You feel not the old chime,
But as I sit, gazing at its smile,
At home, I felt; a friend so sublime.

60. Sink In

When does it sink in –
The thing in front of you?
The air that you now breathe –
Is of a place that's new.
Uprooted from your solace,
From a place so homely home,
A place so safe and bubbled –
And in it, you would freely roam.
You land on a place uneasy,
But a weak heart, you do not possess,
A soul so bright and an aura alluring,
Of every walk of life, you impress.
Let not your fear ruin your fate,
Let not your discomfort pull you back –
From emerging victoriously strong –
And imbibe in you all that you lack.

61. Your People

The time takes a nasty turn,
The gates of despair open wide,
At a time so heinously harsh –
A shoulder, your people provide.
Laugh, cry, share or be quite –
It matters not what you do,
Simply stay in their warm vicinity –
Like on a soft petal, a drop of dew.
The true ones would never judge,
Your presence they indeed cherish,
Take time out for these true gems –
For nary a knows, when they perish.

62. Torn

A moment so ghoulish –
When a choice is to be made,
An apple or an orange, but for one –
The other you would never trade.
Love for both,
Attached with both,
But one despises the other,
This dilemma you so loath.
Day in and day out –
You hope they get along,
None can change what they are –
For 'tis why this chasm prolongs.
A chasm so deep and eerie,
The cracks at first did warn,
You stand still strong –
For an eternity was sworn,
You hope your grip is strong –
So, in holding both, you don't get torn.

63. Patience

Is it a cancer that slowly kills?
Or is it what makes one strong?
Does it help in swallowing sour pills?
Or in trusting it, we all are wrong?
Hard to trust this thing; patience,
At times it blinds us on a path –
So spookily surreal and uncertain,
One fears fate's likely wrath.
But if not it, then what?
For at times so helpless,
Shackled limbs and shaken faith,
Patiently progress, nonetheless.
Taking all the hideous hits,
A time so rough and longueur,
Patiently trust and follow your wits,
Through such times, one comes out stronger.

64. Open Arms

Bound so tight –
By man-made musts,
A moment of joy –
Is covered with dust.
Dust that blows –
By society's stomps –
On what they perceive as icky –
For they fear the locust swamps.
A smile or laugh –
They perceive it a sin,
"How can you have fun –
When we lived a life in tin?"
So now they curb the younger –
And call it a moral's win.
Bound so tight –
I dimmed my charms,
Closed, in every way –
I struggle to open my arms.

65. Rural Charms

On the terrace –
On a night so dark,
City lights so far –
Giving off a scintillating spark.
Amidst all the pure and fresh,
Drizzles and breeze deodorizing the flesh,
I stand surrounded by a serene silence –
As all of nature comes into a mesh.
A mesh so soporific,
Like a baby in a mother's arms –
I close my eyes to its gentle dabs,
Oh, what a heaven; the urban charms.

66. Wander

To sleep on a bed –
That is not mine,
To breathe an air –
So pure and divine,
To capture moments –
So precious and fine,
These are the things –
One's life that design.
The night before –
A journey begins,
A plethora of emotions –
So surreally spins,
I picture myself on a beach –
Or swimming deep with my fins –
Or trekking the tallest summits –
Freezing my palms and chins.
An unplanned venture,
A destination unknown,
A bag lightly packed –
A few pairs that I own,
All that I'd experience –
That must have had minds blown,
I wonder with a dim light –
For tomorrow I shall wander alone.

67. Dubious Digs

A point, promising –
On a land above oil,
He dug a few feet –
Then jumped to the next soil.
An audacious man –
With an impatient heart,
A "few feet" is never enough –
If with a fortune you wish to depart.
How deep does one go –
Before they see hope?
Hope demands trust –
As one climbs up a rope.
A point, promising –
On a land above oil,
If the dig one resumes –
Their fortune they would not spoil.

68. Something Else

A seed they sowed,
Love, care and protection,
Worked sweats as they ploughed –
For its fruit ought to have perfection.
Red, juicy, firm and symmetric,
An apple such is rare,
To place all bets on a delicate seed,
It is an act cruel and unfair.
Apples it is, that you love,
You know not the seed you sowed,
This seed bears no apples –
And on it, a load is bestowed.
A load to yield the impossible,
For this seed would bear a peach,
That is what it's meant for,
To be something else, it must not screech.

69. A Walk through Time

Rather being on wheels -
I walk on this road,
With every step I take -
I wonder how its time flowed.
A decade ago -
Along this road -
Perhaps an elegant -
Greener view it showed.
A century ago -
On this land,
The useless countless -
Wars it had.
To think of how it unfolds,
Growth, prosperity, and life,
A walk instead of wheels -
Glimpsed me of this road's life.

70. Death Seduces

It whispers into you —
A temptation so vehement,
Like a deadly siren —
Who loves to torment.
Your oaths and pledges,
Punches in the water —
Hoping to make a dent,
Tons have fallen to its slaughter.
A moment's pleasure it gives,
Being between your fingers —
As you take it to your lips,
With a devil's smile, it lingers.
Its ashes fall down —
Along with your time,
Seeing you, your soul frowns —
For against it, you commit this crime.

71. Spit Out

Why, oh precious, do you suffer?
Suffer that nary a person knows of,
Why do you let it torture and kill?
With a brave face, your pain, you shove.
You protect none with isolation,
Werewolves are but a myth,
A human is meant to feel,
Curbing it fosters a lethal labyrinth.
Look at you, so dingy and dull,
The venom you conceal sucks off you —
All that's pure, precious, and bright,
The color that describes you is blue.
Spit out what your demons whisper,
To scar you is what they desire,
So, say what you ought to say,
Hold not in what dims your fire.

72. I Owe it to Him

I saw him worried –
A part of him losing hope,
For he sees me now,
With this path, I struggle to cope.
I struggle as do others,
Like headless hens –
Who know not why,
We're sealed in our designated dens.
A struggle, if it were chosen,
Chosen by one's own heart,
Perhaps a head, one hen would have,
Chose not a path with a blindfolded dart.
I saw him worried,
A sweet little lad –
With eyes full of dreams,
A cornucopia of magic he had,
I owe him his faith in himself,
For, after all, I am his dad.

73. Subaqueous

Takes a ton to finally dive,
Dive into the dubious depths,
Depths that assure not life,
You count your blessings and breaths.
The dive at first is unbearable –
Like a fish thrown out of the sea,
Limbs and legs swaying in a vacuum –
Until you acclimate and finally see,
See a world that otherwise was vivid,
'Tis worth the dive, you would agree.
Creatures unheard of and unseen –
An amateur would never apprehend,
In abandoning the land, only a few lean,
To follow the "safe" others intend,
Of a venture less ventured who are keen –
May taste the nectar in the end.

74. Back At It

The sun scintillatingly shines –
Like it is on cloud nine,
All around is good and pure –
Yet I lazily lay supine.
I know not what to call it –
That engulfs one in its pit –
Once their ebullience extinguishes,
The workaday, they are back to it.
The merriment moments spent –
Reshapes what has been bent,
For one often deserves a break –
So, the workaday, they do not resent.

75. A Dew of Fantasy

Oh, thee reality, so heartless,
The devil's pawn in disguise,
Those who endure your hits —
Are hailed and seen as wise,
And those who sulk and crib —
Seal their ardor's demise.
Of all those fallen fervors —
Some scintillatingly shone —
Before the hits overpowered —
And cornered them in a dingy zone,
For fantasy, they zealously desired,
To heartbreaks, it makes one prone.
The thin fine line —
Between reverie and hope,
'Tis where it coldly lies —
Reality's ruinous rope,
From which I wish to cut my ties —
And with a dew of fantasy, forever elope.

76. Shapeless Bliss

This thing is one –
That none can define,
Peace, pleasure, and paradise,
An entity so divine,
And in its alluring abyss –
Souls serenely entwine,
As they did, over this time,
Souls, yours and mine,
And despite some noxious qualms –
They continue to shine,
Shine brighter than the sun –
As we let them not confine,
For entities so delicately strong –
Only when free, can refine,
A shapeless bliss is this thing called Love,
Its heavenly beauty has many a design.

77. For Granted

Clinging to souls –
That are not yours,
Poking in them holes –
To stringing them to yours,
'Tis not how love strolls –
Nor an eternity it ensures.
The fear you carry,
A chasm it creates.
What truly is scary –
Is you being stuck behind the gates.
The gates that make you viciously wary,
Beware of those demons' baits.
All this while your soul screams,
Screams, for you desire all but it,
It is one that for you so gleams,
But its gleam you often shove in a pit.
To thy own self –
You are scarcely there,
Like precious pearls on a shelf –
It is heeded to, but oh so rare,
Enervating and shrinking in itself,
It needs from you better care.
All, but you, praise this soul,
For facets not fungible in it are planted.

So perhaps 'tis time, thy soul thee extol,
For decades you took it for granted.

78. Bite Through

Spooky chuckles startle,
My soul freezes and thaws –
Again and again till its numb,
This darkness mercilessly gnaws.
Silence of the perished –
Or was it of the emptiness,
Knew not of the direction nor of the destiny,
A step at a time is a success –
But each more daunting than the last,
That renders my hope in distress.
A force keeps pulling me back –
From what may lay ahead,
Its words and intent seem pure –
But my intent to advance is still not dead.
A part of my soul sees a light –
At the end of this harrowing hole,
But with Angels holding my hand tight,
So far, nary a scratch on my soul,
Demons dare and strike for sure –
To break and mold one at their whim,
But what they hurt can be cured,
Your angels would let not your light dim.

79. I Love You, But Please Leave

Befuddled me, I greet thee,
Like a child meets a kinsfolk —
Distantly familiar, not so loving,
But seeing you makes me choke.
Many a time, you have kept me —
From arenas I "should not" visit,
Many a time, you shoot me in the knee —
So I don't fall into a potential pit,
But perhaps, myself, I ought to see —
All the world, and not be in limit,
You wander in my mind —
Like a venomous frog in a well,
Your intentions may be purely kind —
But I fear being sealed in my shell,
For I wish to freely find —
Myself, and not regret or dwell.
The worst may yet come,
For I know not of any pits,
But you're never leaving, are you?
So, hold me when you see me in fits.
Oh, thee dubious dementors,
You care for me, I believe,

But let me heed my minacious mentors,
I love you, but for now, please leave.

80. An Anchor

The limbs hardly move –
For my burning brittle spine –
Renders me blisteringly burnt out,
But "bravely," I say "I'm fine!",
I open up a nutshell –
And find in it another shell,
A never-ending cycle propels –
That renders me in a dubious dwell,
It whisks me into a venomous well –
That opens up to the gates of hell.
There I see the freakily familiar –
The demons waving and smiling,
I knew them more than they knew me –
For in me, all my life, they have been piling.
Despite being worlds apart,
My soul, they have been beguiling.
Dancing with the demons,
You are blissfully bereaved,
But an anchor one surely needs,
So, from your hell, you can be received.

81. Firefly, a Hope

Amidst the opaquely dark,
As the heart briskly beats,
Not a hiss, roar, or bark,
Every atom in my body heats.
The soul shrinks —
For it sees nothing,
Just before there presents hope —
A flying shining thing.
This thing wanders at night,
A tiny glowing living moon,
In the dark, it will give you sight —
So, you shall not swoon.
'Tis a delicate being,
It fears your fears,
Things such are prone to fleeing,
To the calmly composed, it gladly appears.
Let not your knee jerk —
Scare away this ray of hope,
Offer a welcoming smile; it works,
And it shall even help you elope.

82. The Constant Change

A soul so safely kept –
Exposed to the sinful,
A change one ought to accept,
For a perfect world is wishful.
Breakfast in bed,
Not any more,
A place you ought to head,
Like a sailor off the shore,
For what does not render you dead,
Renders you with a stronger core.
The soul, safely kept,
Lots to learn and teach,
For all the days it will have wept,
Many a mile it shall reach.
So boldly board the new and strange,
The only thing constant in life is change.

83. A Bird in Hand and One in Pocket

A bird in hand –
And one in the pocket,
Which one do you feed?
For you do not fairly split,
The one who is not paid heed –
Perishes in the shunned pit.
The toll on you –
To cater to both,
To neither being true,
What is worth thy oath?
In the end, it might be you –
Who yourself will loathe.
To the bird paid no heed,
Is it indeed fair?
It matters not if later you feed –
For 'tis now that it needs your care,
With false hope do not lead,
Rather release it in the air.

84. Pandora Unboxed

The lion tastes the blood –
And so begins the thirst,
The cracked dams unleash a flood –
That purifies all the curst,
The petals, alas unfurl from the bud –
To do so, they were scared at first.
So is that what lies within –
All of us, a felicitous flair,
Sealed and locked as one grows,
It would rather vanish in thin air,
As did Rapunzel, from her tower –
For the world needed her golden hair,
Take not thy blessing for granted –
For 'tis something to carefully care.
Life gives all –
More than a few chances –
To hold on to or fall –
From where thy ascend commences,
'Tis upon one to make the call –
Whether to stay within the fences,
For it demands a big bad brawl,
But life, later, is worth the expenses.

85. Unquenched

In an ocean so pure —
He swims in thirst —
Which exalts in his blind tour,
A fate so curst.
Drowning in his vanity,
Brewing a vexatious view —
That corrupts his sanity,
This toxic cycle is not new.
This mistake, millions made,
To pay no heed to what is in front.
Like a candle of hope slowly fades,
So does the unheeded that is in front.
Now, out of breath,
In an ocean so pure, entrenched,
Moronically drowning to his death,
In an ocean so pure, unquenched.

86. Boomeranging Bonds

The heartless dawn mocks,
Showing up as wonted,
Like a cold parent preaches,
A forever hug I wanted.
'Tis a small world –
Yet the distance stings,
A beloved, seen from afar,
Oh, the urge to cry and cling.
I lay on the cold floor –
To soothe my burning soul,
'Tis not enough; I need more,
More of them; exalted is this hole,
I fear the sting will soon sore,
But these demons are what I ought to control,
The lion within can still roar,
And soon again, you shall be whole.
Look up at the stars –
At night, so alluring,
Perhaps they see the same star –
A moment so precious and curing.
Sometimes it demands to be afar,
A love so pure, forever, maturing.

87. A Dew from Heaven

Amidst the waste, in rags,
This man cleans for a penny.
A sight so sour but real,
For lives like these are many.
The blissful beauty of youth —
Tarnished to the turns of time.
The one you see now is uncouth,
Was once a soloist sublime.
Yodeling through the scraps,
Gazing toward heaven for hope.
As his soul woefully wraps,
A dew from heaven descends a hope.

88. The Circle that Binds

She set her eyes one fine day,
A day so pure and endearing,
Among the riches, I was in display,
She spent a while, merrily leering.
A beautiful woman in her prime,
The urge in me to bind her to one,
One who'd make her forget time –
And fill her life with frolic and fun.
On the days that followed –
I laid with grace in my case,
Curiously rooting and hoping that –
Her partner is one who'd truly embrace.
The day had finally come,
How magical a venue it was.
But why was she so low and numb?
I sat beside her, wondering the cause.
The one to make her forget time –
Had left her for reasons chauvinist.
A pretty little lass in her prime,
Just me and her, and the world in mist.
I lay now on her finger,
She turns me over in despair,
Our souls bound, just me and her,
A vow I made to love her and care.

89. A Thing of Peace

Raindrops on the babbling brooks,
Cuddling of the waves and shores,
A view so serene, none forsook,
For a thing of peace, one truly adores.
The scent of earth, fresh and rich,
The warmly cold breeze in the air,
Jovially alive, the flora on the ditch,
Pearls on petals, a beauty so rare.
I look up to the mizzling grey sky —
With dim eyes, I receive its bounty,
To its gentle dominance, I merrily comply,
Like a precious pup, delightfully dainty.
Hopping about the ponds and puddles,
Like an elated doe in blissful meadows,
I brush my palms against all I can,
That sucks off me all my woes.
The sprinkling on the pebbles,
A melodious melody it makes.
To its enchantment, I so revel,
As, to a tune, does a wild snake.
At last, I submit to the rays —
As I lay on the earth, warmly wet.
The soul within craves such days,
A thing of peace, all ought to get.

90. A Seed was Sown

A seed was sown –
Inside a cave.
Its magic never shown,
'Tis a precious thing to save.
Cared for and nurtured –
Such that none received.
To be one, rough and tough,
Only in theory it perceived.
A seed was sown –
In a comfortable camp.
How brightly it shone,
Like a firefly in a lamp.
The fruits it would bore,
Rare, beautiful, and sweet.
A curious craving in its core,
To abscond the comfort and bear the heat.
A seed was sown –
Within warm walls.
How strong it could have grown,
Among the droughts and squalls.
Oblivious to the world outside,
A blissfully ignorant smile it wears.
Many a plant, in solace, have died,
For one survives if only one dares.

91. A Pluto

The one not like the rest,
The one called out last,
The odd one out in a fest —
And deviant from its cast.
With high hopes and dreams —
It jovially joined a group.
The initial phase, sugars, creams,
With time, it decamped the troop.
Cries of hell hoping to flood out,
But dammed by the insecure hound.
Like a plant trying to bud out,
Weighed down by a rock on the ground.
Now it sees, from a far-off place,
Yet staying put at its assigned place,
Hoping in them there is still its trace —
So never from their lives does it truly efface.

92. The Other Half

Clouds clapped in a fit of pique,

The world around grew grey and dark,

Among the drenched and empty streets –

A jovial young boy, with a soulful spark.

A smile, such that never seen before,

Hopping about like twinkle toes,

Save a few spots, nary a thing he wore,

Sucking the nectar, he surely knows.

The crowd with suits and shoes,

The first to sprint, under or inside –

A shelter or their ivory homes,

To what they'd miss, they're so blind.

A graceful smile at the rainbow,

But in a natural pool, a foolish laugh.

I saw them both, and now I know,

The beauty in the lives of the other half.

93. Why?

"Heads up," said I –
To the headless chicken,
As a pole, it ran by.
Its plight so sickened.
A zealous fellow on a cliff,
Almost fell off into the abyss,
Jovially traipsing, smoking a spliff,
In terms of sight, he was amiss.
A soldier expressed both –
Raging wrath and sobbing sorrow,
A conflict between love and oath,
From his target, as kids, notes he would borrow.
Some know not their path,
Some know not of what they try,
They drench in an unclean bath,
And are clueless when asked, "Why?"

94. A Love so Pure

On that isle, she merrily stood,

Awaiting the one who completes her.

Recalling the memories, pure and good,

Making the butterflies in her belly stir.

Memories reflecting strength,

Memories reflecting love,

Memories of going to colossal lengths,

For their bond made them overcome.

The many who objected,

The few who cherish,

Above all, they had trajected,

So, this day, they could relish.

On that isle, they together stood,

To each other, they held great allure.

A beautiful kiss she gave to her woman,

An alliance so great and a love so pure.

95. A Bunch of Beautiful Brains

What a bunch of beautiful brains,
That perceives the world in a way –
Unfathomable by the snobbishly sane,
Even in a storm, in glee, they'd sway.
The lord did whisk out the sly –
From these magnificent souls,
For true as the truth itself are they,
But sadly, are exiled to a heinous hole.
Learn from them to talk to a plant,
Not just water them out of duty.
There is magic in their every chant,
The sane, sadly, doesn't fathom the beauty.
Nary an obstacle to their vision,
Most fascinating story they weave.
To the sanely lame, they suggest imprecision,
They're way superior, I hope they believe.

96. Along the Sea

The waves, gently, touch and go –
And leave behind a jewel of the sea.
Like a child comes to its mom and goes –
Leaving on her lap a toy, in glee.
To every jewel, she slightly smiles,
For the sea sees her pain and sorrow.
It might have searched a million miles,
And yet will search again tomorrow.
She stands here on the shore all-day –
With her feet, in the sand, half-buried.
Ruing with all her soul, that wretched day –
When along the sea her man got carried.

97. Another Venture

I shot across the moon –
For I wished not to settle.
To valiant ventures, I always swoon –
And never stop honing my mettle.
To land on the stars,
'Tis a spiritless scheme.
Conquer that thou desire,
Relish the conquered cream.
What eagerly awaits you is limitless –
For the universe remains unexplored.
Let it not swap you for someone less,
Many a time, to you, it has implored.
I shot across the moon –
For I wished to conquer more.
A rough route could be a big boon,
Muster thy will and set off the shore.

98. Innocently Inclusive

They are never waved back at —
Yet to every bird or animal they wave.
They care not of the pretty, ugly, thin, or fat.
Every ant on their path they try to save.
Inquisitively scintillating eyes —
Trying to look beyond the sane.
A pebble could be a miniature moon —
Could never be hunched a "mature" brain.
They drag us by our fingers —
To include us in their fantasies.
Oh, their fantasies and riveting zingers!
Just nod and repeat their jingles,
And witness the endearing ecstasies.
Looking for someone to share it with,
For they wish not to live a life reclusive.
For once, let go of the "grown-up" myth,
And pitch in with the innocently inclusive.

99. A Beacon of Hope

Sentenced to be drenched under a waterfall –
For hours on a frosty winter night.
A burning candle in a hut far off,
A queer warmth in him did it ignite!
An almost defeated mighty king –
In a cave learned a salient lesson.
"Till the heart beats thee still in the ring"
Said the spider while ascending in aggression.
A sharpshooter lost his right hand –
Could now compete or dissolve in sand.
His peers competed with their best hands,
As Karoly won using his only hand.
The summit that you wish to ascend,
A spine-chilling elevated slope.
Your audacious will shall not bend,
Trust the Lord's Beacon of Hope.

100. Against the Stream

Against the stream, he boldly rows,
Like a stallion paving its own turf,
Welcoming all that life throws,
He yodels along his minacious surf.
Along the stream, he had rowed for long,
Its monogamy spurred serious repulsion,
To this side of the stream, he did not belong,
The stream less taken is filled with frisson.
The power of this stream is exalted,
What it demands, he cannot fathom,
It will peel off his skin but coats better ones –
As he crosses the bridge across the chasm.
The ones around would not get,
For they see him "running to his death,"
To undermine him, they shall regret –
When their lives they recall in their final breaths.
This stream is not for the rigid,
For it will bend you to its will,
Though it has a side not frigid,
For all the bends and rigorous drills –
Glorious glory awaits you on that hill,
So boldly fare against the stream,
For the stream less taken is worth the gleam.

www.ingramcontent.com/pod-product-compliance
Lightning Source LLC
Chambersburg PA
CBHW020611160726
47991CB00002BA/732